WE THE PEOPLE

African-Americans in the Colonies

by Jean Kinney Williams

Content Adviser: Stephanie Davenport, Ed.D.,
Director of Education, DuSable Museum of African-American History, Chicago

Reading Adviser: Dr. Linda D. Labbo,
Department of Reading Education, College of Education,
The University of Georgia

COMPASS POINT BOOKS

Minneapolis, Minnesota

Compass Point Books
3722 West 50th Street, #115
Minneapolis, MN 55410

Visit Compass Point Books on the Internet at *www.compasspointbooks.com* or e-mail your request
to *custserv@compasspointbooks.com*

Photographs ©: Hulton/Archive by Getty Images, cover, 3 (middle), 6, 10, 17, 19, 36 (bottom),
41; The Jamestown Yorktown Foundation Collection, Williamsburg, Va., 3 (top), 4, 8; North
Wind Picture Archives, 3 (bottom), 15, 21, 26, 27, 32; National Park Service, Colonial National
Historical Park, 5; Giraudon/Art Resource, N.Y., 7; Gianni Dagli Orti/Corbis, 11; Bettmann/
Corbis, 13, 22, 23; Stock Montage, 16, 36 (top), 38; National Portrait Gallery, Smithsonian
Institution/Art Resource, N.Y., 18; The Connecticut Historical Society, Hartford, Connecticut, 25;
Courtesy of the Florida Museum of Natural History, University of Florida, 29, 31; Courtesy of the
Massachusetts Historical Society, 33; Rare Book and Special Collections Division, Library of
Congress, 34; Courtesy of the American Antiquarian Society, 39.

Editors: E. Russell Primm, Emily J. Dolbear, Sarah E. De Capua, and Catherine Neitge
Photo Researcher: Svetlana Zhurkina
Photo Selector: Linda S. Koutris
Designer/Page Production: Bradfordesign, Inc./The Design Lab
Cartographer: XNR Productions, Inc.

Library of Congress Cataloging-in-Publication Data

Williams, Jean Kinney.
  African-Americans in the colonies / by Jean Kinney Williams.
     v. cm. — (We the people)
Includes bibliographical references and index.
Contents: Jamestown, Virginia, 1621—Slavery becomes an American institution—Recreating
Africa in America—Freedom at any cost—Liberty, but not for all.
  ISBN 0-7565-0303-5
  1. Slavery—United States—History—Juvenile literature. 2. African Americans—History—To
1863—Juvenile literature. 3. United States—History—Colonial period, ca. 1600–1775—Juvenile
literature.
  [1. Slavery. 2. African Americans—History—Colonial period, ca. 1600–1775. 3. United States—
History—Colonial period, ca. 1600–1775.]
  I. Title. II. We the people (Compass Point Books)
  E446 .W68 2002
  306.3'62'097309033—dc21   2002002956

TABLE OF CONTENTS

JAMESTOWN, VIRGINIA, 1621

"Antonio, a Negro," wrote the **census** taker for Jamestown, Virginia, the first permanent English colony in North America. Antonio, a black man, was a slave. Jamestown desperately needed him and other slaves and servants to work in its tobacco fields. The colony depended on tobacco for its very survival.

Jamestown was founded in 1607 by English settlers. They had been hired by the Virginia Company of London, England, to find riches such as gold on the mysterious

A slave helps a Jamestown farmer load tobacco onto his oxcart.

4

Jamestown residents carry the bodies of dead colonists away from their settlement.

continent of North America. The first several years in Jamestown were difficult. Most of the first settlers who landed there died from starvation or disease.

But the survivors, as well as others who continued to sail across the Atlantic Ocean from England to Jamestown, discovered tobacco would grow in the Virginia soil. That was as good as gold. The people of England bought as much tobacco as the colonists could grow. The problem was finding enough workers to help grow it, harvest it, and prepare it for shipment to England.

Jamestown farmers harvesting the tobacco crop

Men and women who lived in England and didn't have jobs or faced time in jail for having committed a crime could go to Virginia as indentured servants. A tobacco farmer, for example, would pay for a servant's trip to Jamestown in exchange for seven years of labor. After seven years, and if the servant didn't die from overwork or disease, he or she was set free.

There was no slavery in early Jamestown, though its settlers were familiar with the practice. In the **West Indies**

6

and South America, Spanish, Portuguese, and Dutch settlers had been using slaves for several **decades.** The European settlers tried making the local **natives** slaves, but the natives had little resistance to European diseases. Many died or escaped. Then the Europeans began importing slaves from Africa. When the English settled the island of Barbados (in the West Indies) in the early 1600s, they used African slaves to grow and produce sugar. Like tobacco, sugar made adventurous settlers rich.

Slaves pressing the sugar out of sugarcane in South America

AFRICANS ARRIVE IN JAMESTOWN

The first black people in Jamestown were a group of Africans from Bar-bados. They were brought there by Dutch traders in 1619. English-man John Rolfe then bought them. The blacks probably spoke English and, like English indent-ured servants, might eventually have earned their freedom.

"Antonio, a Negro" arrived in Jamestown in 1621. He was owned by the Bennett family, who

John Rolfe checks his tobacco crop.

8

praised his hard work and loyalty. Antonio married a black woman named Mary. Antonio eventually earned his and his family's freedom. He became a landowner and changed his name to Anthony Johnson. He hired a black servant named John Casor. By 1651, thirty years after arriving in Virginia, Anthony Johnson owned 250 acres (101 hectares) of land on Virginia's eastern shore. Every time he hired an indentured servant, he received more land.

In the early days of Jamestown, settlers didn't use the words *white* or *black* to describe themselves. They would refer to themselves or each other as *English, Christian,* or perhaps *servants,* who could be either white or black. Anthony Johnson enjoyed the same rights, freedom, and respect as any white servant who became successful by working hard.

As tobacco farms became bigger, however, the need for laborers grew. Also, the number of English people willing to come to America as indentured servants was shrinking. Sometimes, the colonists tried forcing Native Americans into work, but that was no more successful than it had been in the West Indies. The idea of using African slaves began to spread in Virginia and throughout the colonies, which at that time included all the land along the Atlantic Ocean between Massachusetts and Virginia. While indentured servants were usually either European or African, slaves were drawn from one group: the Africans. Two hundred years of slavery in America had begun.

Slaves rolled barrels of tobacco into sheds, where the tobacco was later dried.

SLAVERY BECOMES AN AMERICAN INSTITUTION

Slavery was not new to people from Africa, where warring tribes often turned prisoners into slaves. In Africa, slaves lived and worked with the family who owned them. Slaves were considered unequal, but they were treated like other family members. This is similar to the experiences of early slaves in America, who worked alongside their white (and sometimes black) owners and

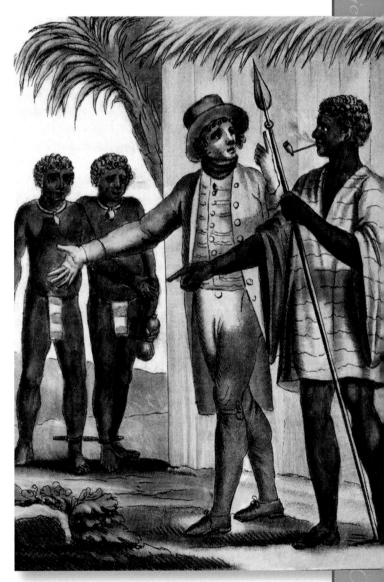

Trading slaves on the African coast

11

probably slept in the same house.

The first Africans in North America had spent time among Europeans in the West Indies. They could speak English and often converted to Christianity. They sometimes won freedom by claiming that, as Christians, they deserved it. Or, they bought their freedom with money they had earned in their free time. By the mid-1600s, one in five black people in North America was free.

As the number of Africans in the colonies increased, however, the laws regarding slavery became stricter. In 1639, Maryland ruled that being Christian did not give slaves the right to be free. In 1641, Massachusetts became the first North American colony to declare slavery a legal **institution.** In 1663, a Virginia court ruled that a child born to a female slave was also a slave. In 1691, marriage between white people and black people became illegal. In general, laws were passed to make it more difficult to set slaves free. In addition, in New Amsterdam (which later became New York), Dutch settlers used slaves to clear the land and make it more inviting for European settlers.

New England, where Africans made up a tiny portion of the population, was the exception. There, few laws restricted the rights of blacks, whether they were free or slaves.

A man in New Amsterdam bargains for slaves.

13

The English colonists' racial attitudes toward the Africans living among them changed as the black population began to grow. In Jamestown, Hugh Gwynn's three indentured servants—two white and one black—ran off to Maryland. When they were returned to Gwynn, all three men were whipped. The white servants were punished by having to work more years as servants before they would be set free. The black servant, a man named John Punch, was told he "shall serve his said master . . . for the time of his natural life." John Punch would never be free. He became a slave.

As the Europeans moved farther west, the demand for laborers increased. In the South, a colony settled in the 1660s called Carolina became the hungriest for new workers. (Carolina was later divided into northern and southern colonies.) Settlers who moved from Barbados to Carolina immediately planned to use African slave labor to develop farmland. This was different from the North American settlers, who turned to black slavery only when

14

The Ashley River flows through South Carolina, where colonists needed slave labor to grow rice and indigo.

white labor became scarce.

African slaves entered Carolina the same way they entered the other colonies—from the West Indies. They usually spoke English, and they enjoyed some privileges in their life of hard work. Those privileges did not last long in Carolina, however, when it was discovered that rice was

15

Slavery was introduced to America in the seventeenth century.

an ideal crop for the low-lying land that surrounded the port city of Charles Town (present-day Charleston).

In both Carolina and Virginia, growing rice and tobacco became big business, and farms gave way to **plantations.** Soon, there were not enough English servants or slaves from Barbados to do the work. So, slaves were brought directly from Africa to the busy slave ports of Charles Town and the Chesapeake Bay areas of Virginia

16

and Maryland. Ships were designed to carry hundreds of slaves at a time. By the end of the 1600s, Africans worked on plantations from Maryland south through Carolina. As the black population in the colonies grew, white lawmakers made it harder for Africans to prosper.

Once, a slave like Anthony Johnson could earn his freedom and live a good life if he worked hard. Now, the land he knew was vanishing. Africans, like John Punch, were seen just one way—as permanent slaves, the property of their owners.

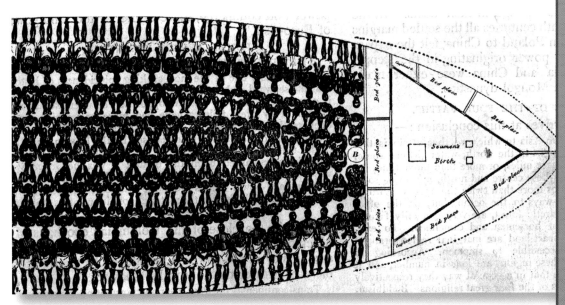

Hundreds of slaves were crowded into a single slave ship.

RE-CREATING AFRICA IN AMERICA

Eleven-year-old Olaudah Equiano was still alive, though sometimes he wished he were not. Born in 1745, he and his sister were kidnapped from their African home by black slave traders. Equiano was heartbroken when he and his sister were separated just after their capture. "I cried continually," he wrote later. He was marched west and was repeatedly sold to other slave traders, until he reached the west coast of Africa, known as the Slave Coast.

Olaudah Equiano

18

There, Olaudah saw white slave traders for the first time. Not knowing who they were, he was terrified that the strangers planned to eat him!

Olaudah was about to take what was called the Middle Passage, the long trip by sea from Africa to North America. The Middle Passage was one part of the slave trade. English slave traders traveled to Africa (called the First Passage) and bought slaves to be sold in American

Traders chained slaves before putting them below deck.

19

colonies (the Middle Passage). Once in North America, the traders then bought goods and products from the colonists to sell in England (called the Last Passage). Conditions on the slave ships were cramped and foul. Many slaves and some white sailors died along the way. Olaudah wished for death to end his fear and heartache, but he survived. He became one of thousands of Africans brought to North America in the 1700s.

Life was difficult for those slaves who came directly from Africa. They did not speak English, and they worked long hours on rice and tobacco plantations. They had few chances to learn other skills besides farming. White people, especially in the South, became more fearful of the Africans as their numbers grew. When South Carolina became an English colony, its population of 18,000 people included 12,000 Africans. Whites used fear, and sometimes severe punishment, to control black slaves.

On large plantations, slave cabins were sometimes miles away from the master's house. As blacks from differ-

Rice barges being unloaded

ent parts of Africa came together in the colonies, they began sharing their music and religious beliefs. One way owners tried to erase the Africans' culture was by giving them English names. Slaves called each other by their African names, however. They were married or buried according to the wedding or funeral customs of their homelands. They

21

Slaves often danced and sang together after a long day on the plantation.

made drums to beat familiar rhythms. They danced and spent time together after a long day's work.

Conditions slowly began to improve as the next **generation** of slaves demanded more rights. Family life was important to the Africans. The white slaveowners learned that keeping families together meant fewer slaves would

22

run away. One owner wrote that slaves "love their families dearly, and none runs away from the other."

Slaves wanted more free time. For a while, plantation slaves worked seven days a week. Then they were given Sundays, the traditional day of rest, off from work. Slaves again began growing vegetables or raising chickens to sell and hired themselves out to non-slave owners after finishing their plantation work. By earning extra money, slave parents could improve the way their families ate and lived.

Female slaves sitting by the fireplace

Though it was rare to be a free black in the southern colonies, slaves did not give up trying to become free. Freedom was easier to achieve in the northern colonies, where slave labor played a smaller role in the **economy.** Venture Smith was one slave who met his goal of freedom.

Like Olaudah, Venture was kidnapped in Africa by black slave traders and brought to the Connecticut Colony as a boy. He was born with the name Broteer, but his first owner renamed him Venture. He grew tall and strong, and after a long day's work, he worked even more, to save money to purchase his freedom. When one of his owners abused him, Venture complained to a Connecticut **justice of the peace.** The man apologized, but said in his defense that there were no laws to protect slaves. Finally, at age thirty-six, Venture Smith bought his freedom from his master. He continued to work, however, so that he could purchase freedom for his wife and children.

Freedom was a burning dream that many enslaved blacks never gave up.

Elisha Corey Book

A

NARRATIVE

OF THE

LIFE AND ADVENTURES

OF

VENTURE,

A NATIVE OF AFRICA:

But resident above sixty years in the United States of America.

RELATED BY HIMSELF.

New-London:

PRINTED BY C. HOLT, AT THE BEE-OFFICE.

1798.

Venture Smith's diary tells of the life of a slave in the colonies.

FREEDOM AT ANY COST

A sign in Charleston read:

Charlestown, July 24th, 1769

> TO BE SOLD
>
> . . . A CARGO OF NINETY-FOUR
>
> PRIME, HEALTHY
>
> **NEGROES . . .**

What would become of those "Negro" men, women, and children just arriving from Africa? Most would labor

An ad for a slave sale in a 1744 issue of the Charleston Gazette in the rice or indigo fields of South Carolina's and Georgia's "low country," low-lying land along the Atlantic coast. Others would be taken to the tobacco plantations of Virginia and Maryland. There they would struggle to learn English and adjust to their new surroundings. They were probably heartbroken by their separation from beloved family members. There were Africans and African-Americans (black slaves born in the colonies) who refused to adjust to slavery, even when it meant risking their lives.

Slave owners often lived in fear of rebellions, or uprisings, against them. Thousands of

A slave working on a rice plantation   **27**

Africans arrived in Charleston in the 1730s. In 1739, the rebellion that South Carolina whites feared took place. On September 9, a band of twenty slaves, led by a man named Jemmy, left their owners and headed south. More slaves joined them along the way, and they killed more than twenty white people that day. Most of the slaves were captured near a town called Stono and executed. The rebellion was crushed, but it was a reminder to white colonists that the more slaves were mistreated, the more hatred they felt for whites.

Jemmy and the other slaves were headed to Saint Augustine, Florida, which the Spanish controlled until 1764. The Spanish had said that any slaves who came to Florida would lead a better life. They would still be slaves, but blacks there were allowed to live with their families, were paid wages, and were taught to use guns to help protect Florida from the English.

Francisco Menendez was one slave who escaped to Saint Augustine. He was awarded his freedom after show-

Slaves head for Saint Augustine.

ing bravery during a British attack in 1728. For many years, he led a settlement called Fort Mose, where about 100 slaves and free Africans lived. During another British attack, Menendez again became a hero, and he decided to visit the Spanish king in person to request a reward. While he was sailing to Spain, the English captured his ship, and Menendez was returned to slavery. He was back in Fort Mose by 1752, however. When the English took control of Florida in 1764, the black residents of Fort Mose fled to Cuba with the Spanish.

Escaped slaves also formed small secret settlements, hidden in the mountains or swampy areas of Virginia and South Carolina. Usually they lived in these places for only a year or two before they were discovered. As European settlers continued moving west, it became harder to find places to hide. Escaped slaves also could "hide out" in bigger cities, such as Charleston or New York, where they blended in with the slaves who lived and worked independently of their owners.

Fort Mose was a Spanish settlement where Indians and African slaves found freedom.

31

By the 1760s, a new movement was gaining strength in the colonies. White colonists talked more and more about the cause of liberty, or freedom, from the British. African slaves began to ask, "Shouldn't liberty and equality be for everyone?"

A slave on a homestead in New York

LIBERTY, BUT NOT FOR ALL

"We have no Property! . . . We have no City! No Country! But we have a Father in Heaven, and we are determined. . . ."

That 1773 **petition** from several slaves to the Massachusetts colony govern- ment made a pas- sionate plea for freedom. Elizabeth Freeman, who was called Mum Bett, also petitioned the colony of Mass- achusetts for her freedom, and she won. She based her

Elizabeth Freeman

33

The Declaration of Rights of the Inhabitants of Massachusetts helped Elizabeth Freeman become a free woman.

case on the Massachusetts Declaration of Rights, which stated, "All people are born free and equal." Upon becoming a freed woman, Mum Bett was hired as a housekeeper by the lawyer who had defended her. When she died, she was buried alongside his family members. The inscription on her tombstone called her "the most efficient helper, and the tenderest friend."

African-Americans made important contributions to both the American Patriots and the British fighting against one another in the Revolutionary War (1775–1783). One of the first men to die for the Patriot cause was a runaway

34

Original Thirteen Colonies
Present-day boundaries

Lake Superior

Lake Michigan

Lake Huron

Lake Ontario

Lake Erie

(part of Massachusetts)

N.H.

Battle of Bunker Hill

New York

Mass. ★Boston

Conn. R.I.

N   W   E   S

0   100   200 miles
0   100   200 kilometers

Pennsylvania

New York (New Amsterdam)

Philadelphia • New Jersey

Maryland • Baltimore Delaware

Atlantic Ocean

Virginia

Chesapeake Bay

Jamestown

North Carolina

South Carolina

Georgia   Stono

Charleston (Charles Town)

NORTH AMERICA   • London

West Indies
Barbados   AFRICA

SOUTH AMERICA

Fort Mose
Saint Augustine

slave in Boston named Crispus Attucks.

In March 1770, an angry mob marched up what is today Boston's State Street, led by Attucks, who was half African, half Wampanoag Indian. As a runaway slave, he understood the importance of freedom and was among the first to confront a group of British soldiers. Five men, including Attucks, were killed. They are considered the first Americans to die in the Revolutionary War.

Crispus Attucks

An article telling of the Boston Massacre and the death of Crispus Attucks

36

Three days later, business in Boston came to a halt when a public funeral was held for all five men, who were considered heroes.

The first major battle of the war took place in 1775, near Boston. At the Battle of Bunker Hill, an African-American named Peter Salem was credited with killing Major Pitcairn, an important British officer.

When the war started, General George Washington, who led the Patriots' Continental army, was against recruiting black soldiers to fight. He thought it would anger southern Patriots. He also wondered how blacks could be re-enslaved after the war if they had fought for the Patriots. When the Patriot army needed more soldiers, however, Washington agreed to allow black men, free or slaves, to join his army.

The British offered freedom to American slaves who joined their army. A man named Titus was a runaway slave who helped the British. He killed many important Patriot leaders in New York and New Jersey

37

Peter Salem killed Major Pitcairn at the Battle of Bunker Hill.

38

THREE POUNDS Reward.

RUN away from the subscriber, living in Shrewsbury, i the county of Monmouth, New-Jersey, a NEGRO man, named TITUS, but may probably change his name; h is about 21 years of age, not very black, near 6 feet high; had on a grey homespun coat, brown breeches, blue and white stockings, and took with him a wallet, drawn up at one end with a string, in which was a quantity of clothes. Whoever takes up said Negroe, and secures him in any goal, or brings him to me, shall be entitled to the above reward of *Three Pounds* proc. and all reasonable charges, paid by

Nov. 8, 1775. § JOHN CORLIS.

An ad about runaway slave Titus

before he was shot in the wrist and died from an infection in 1780.

Altogether, about 5,000 black men fought for the Continental army, and many more fled to the British army. All hoped for freedom at the war's end.

39

The cause of liberty inspired many white Americans to think harder about the morality of slavery. Many decided that human beings owning other human beings was wrong. Though slavery was accepted throughout the colonies under British rule, thousands of Africans were freed by their owners after the war ended. Even George Washington freed his slaves. Including the slaves who served in the armies, a total of 100,000 Africans were freed. Vermont became the first state to ban slavery. Virginia banned importing more slaves from Africa.

At the end of the 1700s, the northern states were abolishing slavery. The new Northwest Territory (present-day Ohio, Indiana, Illinois, Michigan, and Wisconsin) was declared to be free. Some southern states made it easier for slave owners to free their slaves. It would take the long and bloody Civil War (1861–1865) to completely abolish slavery in the United States.

Free African-American soldiers fighting for Northern troops in the Civil War

GLOSSARY

census—an official count of all the people living in a country or district

decades—periods of ten years

economy—the way a country runs its industry, trade, or finance

generation—the average amount of time between the birth of parents and that of their children; a generation is said to be about thirty years

institution—a well-established custom or tradition

justice of the peace—someone who hears cases in local courts of law

natives—people who originally lived in a certain place

petition—a serious plea or request to a person or persons in authority

plantations—large farms that specialized in growing one crop

West Indies—a string of islands in the Western Hemisphere that separates the Caribbean Sea from the Atlantic Ocean

42

DID YOU KNOW?

- Slavery has existed throughout the world since people first began recording history—in China, India, the Americas, and ancient Greece and Rome.

- Some of the first travelers to the Americas were African sailors.

- Before slavery became widespread in Virginia, there was such a great need for workers that some people in England were kidnapped and forced to become indentured servants in North America.

- When Georgia was founded in 1733, it was the only non-slave colony in British North America. Then the need for labor made slavery a reality in Georgia, too. In 1750, it was the last of the thirteen colonies to legalize slavery.

- Phillis Wheatley, a Massachusetts slave, arrived in America as a sickly child. A woman named Mrs. Wheatley felt sorry for her and bought her in 1761. She treated Phillis like a daughter. Phillis learned to read and studied literature, history, geography, and astronomy. She became a poet, and a book of her poems was published in London.

IMPORTANT DATES

Timeline

1619	The first Africans arrive in North America.
1641	Massachusetts legalizes slavery.
1663	Virginia rules that children born to a slave woman are considered slaves.
1660s	Carolina is settled, and landowners use slave labor.
1705	The Virginia colonial government declares that all non-Christian servants will be their owners' property.
1739	The Stono Rebellion occurs; Georgia is settled as a non-slave colony.
1750	Georgia is the last colony to legalize slavery.
1770	Crispus Attucks is one of the first Patriots killed by the British.
1778	George Washington decides to recruit blacks for the Continental army.
1783	The American Revolutionary War ends after the British surrender to the Continental army.

IMPORTANT PEOPLE

CRISPUS ATTUCKS
(1723?–1770), *early hero of the American Revolution; killed by British soldiers in Boston in 1770*

MUM BETT
(1742–1829), *Massachusetts slave who sued the colonial government for her freedom; won her case and was freed*

OLAUDAH EQUIANO
(1745–1797), *kidnapped by African slave traders in 1756; earned his freedom in 1766; published a best-selling book about his life in several editions*

FRANCISCO MENENDEZ
(unknown), *slave who ran away to Saint Augustine, Florida, which was under Spanish rule until 1764; brave warrior for the Spanish when they were attacked by the British; awarded with his freedom*

PHILLIS WHEATLEY
(1753?–1784), *slave girl educated by her owner in Massachusetts; had a book of her poems published*

WANT TO KNOW MORE?

At the Library

Ferris, Jeri Chase. *With Open Hands: A Story About Biddy Mason.*
Minneapolis: Carolrhoda Books, 1999.

Kent, Deborah. *African-Americans in the Thirteen Colonies.* Danbury, Conn.:
Children's Press, 1996.

Salisbury, Cynthia. *Phillis Wheatley: Legendary African-American Poet.*
Springfield, N.J.: Enslow Publishers, 2001.

On the Web

History Museum of Slavery in the Atlantic

http://www.jhunix.hcf.jhu.edu/~plarson/smuseum/welcome.htm

To visit a virtual museum dedicated to the history of
slavery and the slave trade in the Atlantic

Through the Mail

The Museum of Afro-American History

14 Beacon Street

Suite 719

Boston, MA 02108

For information on the contributions of African-Americans
during the colonial period in New England

On the Road

Bunker Hill Monument

Boston National Historical Park

Charlestown Navy Yard

Boston, MA 02129

617/242-5642

To visit the monument that commemorates the first

battle of the Revolutionary War, where African-American

Peter Salem killed Major Pitcairn

INDEX

About the Author

Jean Kinney Williams lives and writes in Cincinnati, Ohio. Her nonfiction books for children include *Matthew Henson: Polar Adventure* and a series of books about American religions. She is also the author of *The Pony Express.*